DRIFTWOOD TONES

DRIFTWOOD TONES

Nature Poetry of Beauty and Presence

TERRY-LYNN JOHNSON

Waterside Productions

Copyright © 2023 by Terry-Lynn Johnson
www.lakeheadpoet.com

All rights reserved. This book or any portion thereof may not be reproduced or used in any manner whatsoever without the express written permission of the publisher except for the use of brief quotations in articles and book reviews.

ISBN-13: 978-1-960583-31-4 hardcover edition
ISBN-13: 978-1-960583-13-0 paperback edition
ISBN-13: 978-1-960583-14-7 e-book edition

Waterside Productions
2055 Oxford Ave
Cardiff, CA 92007
www.waterside.com

Dedication

for Faith and Devon

The poem "Season of Old" brings to us the magic of Christmas traditions. The points of constellations sparkle in the clear night sky as we wait expectantly for the prancing of reindeer on the roof and put cookies out on a plate. Children bring joy and love to the Christmas Season and grandchildren sprinkle even more joy and love on top. My Christmas prayer for you is that you meet each challenge with courage and faith while greeting each day with gratefulness. You will enjoy some of the poems in this collection— one of my favourites is "Black Capped Chickadee"— and others will wait until you're older. I hope that you come back to the beauty of the poems in this collection with child-like wonder as seasons pass. And reach for the stars in the clear night sky, knowing that I love you, now and forever.

Table of Contents

Foreword ·xi
Acknowledgement · xiii
Introduction · xv

Pastel Orchid · 1
Rainy Days and Poetry · 2
Writing in the Sand · 3
Morning Prayer · 4
White Clover and Goodbyes · 5
Spring Rain · 6
Countryside Fields · 7
Wintering Romance · 8
Morning Light · 9
Shorelines · 10
Sail Tip on the Horizon · 11
A Note in the Bottle · 12
Blue Heron · 13
Northern Tranquility · 14
Daisy Petals and Fireflies · 15
The Park Bench in Morning Hours · · · · · · · · · · · · · · · 16
Double Song · 17
Crystal Moments · 18
Songbirds · 19
Blue Bird · 20

The Village	21
Morning Coffee	22
Morning Break	23
By the River Bend	24
Canoe Trailer	25
The Innkeeper	26
Reverence	27
The Evening Song	28
Fly to Paris	30
Three Candies for a Cent	31
Blueberry Festival	32
Sundry Sunday	33
Refreshment of Golden Sunset	34
A Note by the Garden	35
The Last Hour	36
Train Station Platform	37
The Cricket and the Moon	38
Summer Storm	39
Citrus and Cloves	40
Burnt Orange Tiger Lilies	41
Rustic Leaves	42
Geese Over the Fall Canvas	43
Fall Season in the Suburbs	44
Fall Trail	45
Meadow Crow	46
Golden Leaves	47
Fair Trade Coffee Shop	48
Reflection in the Window	49
The Winding Road	50
Dormant Branches	51
Wintering Blue Jay	52
Weathered Crosses	53
A Solitary Note	54
Wintered Countryside	55
Winter Walking Trail	56

White Snow Geese	57
Black Capped Chickadee	58
Season Snowfall	59
Season of Old	60
The Donkey	62
Sprigs of Holly	63
The Red Mailbox	64
Forecast of Snow	65
Snow Globe	66
Candlelight Service	67
Old Father Time	68
Snow and Thistles	69
Quarter Note	70
Joy	71
Sit for Tea	72
A Poet and Picker and Friends	73
Company in the Corner	74
Serenity	75
Cherished Moments	76
Reclamation	77
Simply Love	78
Tribute	79
Praise Thy Seasons	81
Greet the Day	83
Index of Opening Phrases	85
About the Author	89

FOREWORD

I confess that I was a little surprised when my former student and fellow teacher entitled her most recent volume of verse *Driftwood Tones: Nature Poetry of Beauty and Presence* (2023, 89 pages). I presently reside on the West Coast and taught her for graduate and undergraduate studies at Lakehead University as an Associate Professor, Faculty of Education, and Adjunct Professor, Department of English. With the setting of the oceanside, "Writing in the Sand" (3) brings us to the driftwood on the shores of the West Coast and Maritimes, but driftwood also occurs (as this volume reminds us) in the Great Lakes basin. Canadian poet Terry-Lynn Johnson was born in Nipigon and was raised in Northwestern Ontario. Her slender volume's seventy-nine lyrics evoke the natural world of the Canadian Shield, the Great Lakes and Sleeping Giant. Imagery associated with wind, sand, birds (many, many species, from Sandpipers to Blue Jays to Chickadees), trees, sky, and water enable the poet to take readers through "the ebb and flow of life" ("Writing in the Sand" line 1). Her style reminds us of the Japanese haiku, with its emphasis on evocative natural scenes that reflect a contemplative, tranquil mood. Sensory appeal (taste, touch, smell, visual and auditory appeal) is everywhere in these lyrics as the poet holds up moments of natural wonder for our enjoyment and speculation. She reminds us that humanity does not live apart from the natural world, but alongside it and, in golden moments, within it. She terms the relationship between the built and natural environments "interconnectedness." Whether she transports us to a railway platform or into the midst of a summer storm, we are always alive to the forces of nature, the times of day, and the vagaries of the seasons. The lyrics often take a page or less— much less in the case of the five-line "Joy" (page 71) and the eleven-word "Reclamation" (page 77). Simple diction, unrhymed verse, natural scenes enshrined in simple yet moving language—that is what Terry-Lynn Johnson's slender volume is all about.

Philip V. Allingham, Ph.D.
Professor Emeritus
Formerly: Faculty of Education, and
Adjunct Professor,
Department of English
Lakehead University

ACKNOWLEDGEMENT

To My Husband
Michael Kivari

Thank you for bringing music to my life.

Introduction

*As the tide washes away the writing in the sand
and leaves driftwood tones in its wake.*
from "Writing in the Sand"

Pastel Orchid

The dove descended
in haze of a morning dream—
With a twig from the blooming orchid
that sits on my kitchen windowsill
from where I look out at the world.
The pastel vibrant against soft mist.
Be still whispered the air
that gently brushed my face
from the descending flight of the dove.
Be still—
know your heart—
and be at peace.

Rainy Days and Poetry

Small birds shelter
with no song.
And the world slows down
to the patter of rain.
The beauty reflected
in beads of raindrops
on feathered backs of birds
sheltered in thickets.
The birdsong is uplifted
with breaking sun
from verdant greens in mist—
Rainy days and poetry
heal the soul.

Writing in the Sand

Trust the ebb and flow of life.
As the tide washes away the writing in the sand
and leaves driftwood tones in its wake.
Tufts of beach grass wave along the oceanside,
as you quietly sit by the shore in salty mist with your thoughts.
Life brings tears to your eyes, both in sorrow and joy.
And the turn of the tide is as sure as the moon
as the beach sands are washed away.

Morning Prayer

Someone is knocking at the door
in the early morning hours.
And someone rang the bell.
Awakened from sleep,
you attune to the quietness
and stillness—
the dog has not stirred.
And you reason
it is nothing more than a dream.
And time for morning prayer.

White Clover and Goodbyes

The scent of white clover
lends sweetness to the breeze
after morning spring rain.
And bees harvest with rays of sun
breaking through clouds of cotton
in the sky—
Yet what is done cannot be
undone—
and I no longer care for
bees and white clover on a
spring morning.
You are gone and you left me
without a goodbye.

Spring Rain

The white throated sparrow nests
in the light spring rain.
The morning mist lifting his mating song
to the heavens,
lending grace to shed tears of goodbye
under solemn skies.
The call beckons towards a wearied
lament for peace—
with the timbre of sad notes
in the spring refrain.

Countryside Fields

The day awakens from slumber
with ruckus in the white pine
at first morning light.
The rural home quiet
with no one left to throw
out the crust of toast for Rosie.
Her cawing clatters over the cherry
blossomed countryside.
And the nightingale pipes
with chittered song over
foreign fields.

Wintering Romance

The snow falls lightly with
the month of April
And small birds shelter
with buoyant mist on feathered wings.
Hopes are dashed with late spring
And romance fails with passing years.
The wintering birds chirrup from
shelter of twined branch—
And tracks criss-cross over pristine snow
With the golden debris of husks and seeds
scattered under birch.

Morning Light

I hear the rain patter outside my window.
But with the cracking of the dawn,
the birds are singing.
And the crow clatters demanding his way
As my neighbour tosses from her front
porch his favourite dish.
I feel like the same person as in my youth—
With perhaps a few more insights
as I gaze out, with the morning fog rising up
and my regrets burning off
with the rising sun.
And, I think of how quickly years pass—
As the morning light lends itself
to a soft mist and a promise of a spring day.
For which I am grateful.

SHORELINES

Strolling along coastal shores,
sandpipers dash on the beach.
The terns breast the coastal wind
just over the waves
And gulls perch on driftwood—
Pause is given to rest
just beyond the old war fortifications
which dot the hillsides—
And as you look out over the horizon,
there is a sense of resignation knowing
that there are some things in life
you cannot change.
The waves cap with salty brine
as the seabirds settle on
the shoreline.

Sail Tip on the Horizon

The white caps splash over
the rocky crag of the morning lake.
And the brown herring gull
coasts the shoreline,
not able to breast the high winds.
As you set sail, you reflect
on your own quest and fortune.
The sail tip a white sliver
on the horizon.

A Note in the Bottle

I thought of you today
with broken longing—
As he walked towards me
with the same stride in his step,
the same build to his frame,
and the quilted plaid of hard work
and hard play.
The drizzling rain left circles of hope
in the puddles.
And the finch's chirp was bittersweet.
He passed by me with cordial exchange
of neighbourly greet.
And I reminisced on our better days
before the bottle's steel grip.

Blue Heron

I am told the rare sighting
of the blue heron is a blessing.
As he stands on the shore with his neck arched,
his one foot propped, and leg tucked.

I always hope to see the heron again.
As it visits the waters of the shore
by the tall marshland grasses,
in quiet hours of early morning and dusk.

Northern Tranquility

With early dawn I stood by the bay
and mist laid low on the lake.
The planks were dampened with dew
and the gentle lapping of waves.
Solaced with the echo, the hallowed echo—
the echo of the northern loon.

I turned from the bay and travelled by path
where wild flowers lay low in morn field abloom,
and, oh, how I wished, I sincerely wished,
I could share such moments with you.
Sitting on the bay dampened by dew
when early morn mists lay low on the lake,
and one hears the echo, the hallowed echo—
the echo of the northern loon.

Daisy Petals and Fireflies

Petals of he loves me,
loves me not,
line diverging pathways.
And life goes separate ways
for most.
But childhood bonds
are treasured.
And I grieved
that you must leave.
Under a blanket of night sky
with radiant stars
and fireflies.

The Park Bench in Morning Hours

Just as the crow awakens the songbird
and harkens dawn—
the rain stops, the fog lifts, and
pathways clear with heavy droplets
resting on green leaves.
Just as sorrows flow and
regrets revisit before stirring from slumber—
faith renews with the note from
the awakening song and its acclamation
that all is well.
Just as the morning breaks from greys
into the light of promise and
the songbirds chorus with the new day—
the park bench remains empty.
As worldly ways keep you too busy
to share your day with a beckoning friend.

Double Song

Weep, weep,
for our brothers and sisters.
Grief, grief,
for our brothers and sisters.
Pray, pray,
for our brothers and sisters.
The skies are blue.
The skies are grey.
The birds praise.
The songbird is under the same
blue and grey skies.

Crystal Moments

Almost every wound heals as time passes.
And, others need acceptance to rest,
giving depths to your rich undertones.
Nurture your soul with crystal moments,
a raindrop, a sunset,
when orange rays kiss the evening sky.
Or when waking at dawn with the first note
of morning song.
Cherish crystal moments that nurture
your wounded soul, with the bit of solace
gained by knowing that in suffering,
there is grace.

Songbirds

Early each dawn
before the bustling city day,
I hear each note of the songbirds.
With this spring it seems
little chickadees are all a chatter and gay.
Yet, one note seems quite a mystery.
I've heard it outside my window,
and I've heard it on the lakeshore—
a nostalgic note,
where one can imagine the smell
of the campfire and the coffee.
You might know of it—
a long low whistle of a note
followed by four short.
Is it maybe a sparrow's call?
How could something so close to my soul
not be known by myself at all?

Blue Bird

Hey Dylan, drop over,
so we can discuss
current events
over morning coffee.
And you can skirt big questions
and refuse an autograph
but grace us with your presence—
as in the end
it all makes no sense
but to add beauty, and music
to changing times.
The blue bird beckons
with a single harmonic
note.

The Village

Last summer we sat in the shade
of the birch tree with chilled iced tea,
sharing light conversation.
The decorative gnomes busy gardening
in the brambles.
Then hard winter came with short days.
And the gnome village lost its magic
under drifts of snow,
with question to why the world is cold.
When the sun came higher
and the drifts melted with fair winds,
the village was toppled and left
untended.
And you are not here to tend to
the village or
to sit in the shade
this summer.

Morning Coffee

I miss you over morning coffee—
when the rich aroma lingers in the kitchen.
And when I clean in the spring as the sun
shines through the window,
revealing the dust that settled on cloudy days.
I miss you when fall bulbs blossom with
bright and pastel shades along bordering gardens,
when grackles visit the lawn in midday,
and when leaves are raked into piles with the fall breeze.
Such moments tug at my soul, but I must let you rest.
The morning sun kisses you good night—
And steam wisps over my white porcelain mug
with freshly ground and brewed coffee.

Morning Break

The robin sits under the sun
on the manicured lawn which sparkles
with morning dew,
surveying the scene while
acknowledging my presence
on the deck, with my
morning coffee and open book.
He scoots, stops, hops, sits,
and then pecks at a green patch
with his golden beak.
His silhouette is still before
sharing a few notes of content.
He sits giving pause to morning tasks
under the warming sun,
with the glistening dew settled
on blades of green grass.

By the River Bend

The soul deepens with sorrow like water in the
still pool on the bend of the river.
And the blue notes of the songbird resonate in
the depths of the green shades,
with the fresh scent of morning rain,
and layered hues in the morning sky.
The brambles of branch bend down to the water.
And while all struggle with knowing their own truth,
the spectrum of tones enhances the beauty of
what can be sensed, with pause
and rest by the riverbank.

Canoe Trailer

The logger planned to paddle cross the lake to fly-fish
in the river, where the beavers build dams
and turtles struggle up banks to lay eggs.
But winds lifted on the lake with rough waves
and birds harboured on the shorelines in grey light.
He settled with morning storm in his cabin with verse
and prose of yellowing twilight—
As bits of vintage crumbled with turn of page.
He made no apology for his resilient faith—
birling down white waters with pike pole
and with light step.
The birds left the shore with late morn and calm lake.
Donning his vest, he paddled cross lake to the mouth
of the river, and upstream to current and undercut,
with hope of a good catch for the day;
returning to his cabin with creel of trout,
under warm smoked hues of sky.

The Innkeeper

The mist rises over the hazed mountain,
and township neighbours begin to stir.
The dogs are walked and morning papers read
with vague foreboding sense of current events.
But for morning hours, all is at peace.
The mist remains low by the old inn,
which sits on the hill beyond the lake waters.
The hues of pinks with rising sun burn off
as the innkeeper contends with business of the day.

Reverence

The offshore landing is framed with weathered logs,
and the sun is blanketed with a soft light,
as smoke from distance hazes the sky.
The dragonfly hovers with plenty to hunt.
And the fish jumps with splash and catch
of translucent wing.
The loon leaves a wake on the still surface of the lake,
as feathered grasses wave in the evening's breeze.
And with the warm hues reflecting on the lake waters,
there is a glimpse of grace,
and a moment of reverence—
as all things come to pass.

The Evening Song

-i-
The planet groans as if in labour pain.
As wide eyed children are tucked in for sleep.
With hope their dreams are filled with
rainbows and cotton clouds, and not of the
fears and anxieties which we try to keep
from their innocence.
Today, I chose love
-ii-
There is a tinge of fear, an unbeknownst
pulse palpated, of what cannot be spoken,
and we resign to trusting peace,
and the good in humanity—
while snippets of truth no longer fill
our appetite or quench our thirst.
Today, I chose charity.
-iii-
We turn to mantras and poets, here and gone.
We turn to God, with fervent prayers,
and with a new painful awareness of
interconnectedness as our planet pains.
Today I chose harmony.

-iv-
Our heart aches with times, and
the worst amid tidbits of news.
Yet, we are blessed and cocooned in a safe
nest while the world weeps.
Today, I chose faith.

-v-
Waves of isolation and unrest, at best,
threaten liberty as we sit on the deck at dark,
sipping red wine and pondering
what tomorrow may bring, when all is done.
Under citronella and patio lanterns.
Today, I chose peace.

-vi-
The moth flies into the flame and drops,
while frogs sing the spring mating song.
Today, I chose hope.

-vii-
We round the sun, and round the sun,
through changing times.

Fly to Paris

With fame and fortune
we shall fly to Paris,
when all is well.
And sit on the boulevard
in a historic café by
the Seine.
Or sit on the bench in the park
under shade—
And, with any luck,
enjoy comradeship
with ghosts of
modernists.

Three Candies for a Cent

We look out at our world
with a jade tint to the lens,
like the thick glass of
a pop bottle,
or the depression glass
salvaged in the thrift store.
And reminisce about when
a bag of mixed up candy
cost a dime.
While framing bohemian values
for minimalist décor.

BLUEBERRY FESTIVAL

Friendships are made
as we sit in the shade
and relish our blueberry pie.
Summer days simple.
Blueberry baskets.

Sundry Sunday

I bravely stepped up to the prairie town
church, with grey plank siding
and white framed windows.
A simple frame.
Inside stood the empty pews—
the one who gave services long left the town
now close to deserted.
Only old farmers still around while tumbleweeds
blow across the dust.
On the altar stood the piano for tune,
not the grandeur.
My footsteps echoed as I stepped inside
and searched for the most simple of faiths.
And tears drew across my face,
knowing the silence of praise.
I gently stepped out of the prairie town church
and sat on the step
while warming sun rays gently caressed,
drying my tears.
Sitting on the church step under the shade
with the most simple of faiths.

Refreshment of Golden Sunset

On the rocks.
As golden as the sunset
and smooth as Santiago's sail.
The muse for an adventurer
who sought solitude
with liquid bronze
in his cabin.

A Note by the Garden

A note is tucked under
the amethyst
along the border of the garden.
As raindrop pearls settle
in mystic light
with translucent hues on wings.
The hummingbird flits by
and then into the branches
of the weeping willow.
Goodbyes are spent—
with a note for you
left by the garden.

The Last Hour

What took you so long?
With the sands of time filtering through,
the silent footstep and the rustle of leaves.
You sat on your bedside, skin ashen grey.
And I pulled a clean shirt over your frail shoulders.
You laboured for breath, and said,
"No birds sing, and there are no squirrels today.
What took you so long?"

If I could save time,
we would spend it under the golden sun.
The birds would sing; the squirrels play.
We would leave the sorrows of this world behind.
But I am left to grieve, to ponder if I knew you not,
through night and through day.
The last hour's sting would lessen, birds would sing,
If I could save time.

Train Station Platform

Travel with the good
with the beginning of a new journey.
And, leave the old baggage
that weighs you down
on the platform as you
board the train.
Leave the old behind as you
steam ahead taking
only your lessons in life.
Leave the old behind
as the train whistles
around the bend of forgiveness.
The thing about old baggage
is one does not remember
what was packed, or why.
Label fragile and let it go.
Let it go and let it be—
As you board the train with
the conductor's last call.

The Cricket and the Moon

Dark clouds hide away the stars—
With chalked notes of dreams
and peace on skies of
blackboard slate.
The cricket chitters in the stillness
of the night—
Under the moon of the solar light
By the hedge bordering
the rock garden.

Summer Storm

The steel sky darkens the forest floor
as ominous shades lend to rich forest greens.
Trunks creek complaint with rising wind.
Small birds silence, and rodents scamper
about thick and rich moss,
as hardy birds hunker down for the storm—
Yet, there is a peaceful lull in the moment.
As the wild lift their heads to smell the scents,
with silhouettes against grey skies, and forest pines.
Standing still beside bulrush, on marshland shores
of stirring lake waters.
As heavy skies rumble of summer rain.

Citrus and Cloves

I harvest cloves of harmony
in my soul.
And scent my home with
the essential oils of
orange blossom,
and citrus.
But heaviness lends to grief
as I pause for prayer.
Let there be peace.

Burnt Orange Tiger Lilies

In front of my childhood home,
the sun warmly caressed
the tiger lily bedding
on the barren lawn.

In front of my childhood home,
pumpkin pie in the oven,
the burnt orange tiger lilies
raged out in the autumn.

In front of my childhood home,
I met with my mother
among pastoral lilies
and forgave her for dying.

Rustic Leaves

He returned to the park, the evening chilled.
The park bench mottled with rustic leaves.
His collar buttoned with the evening breeze.
He hoped to see her again—
as they had sat on the bench in early fall,
with the sun glimpsing through the poplar.
His dog's knowing eyes held his own,
with a slight tail wag,
as he raised his weary bones after sitting some time
to stride down the boardwalk—
With the evening sun over the golden marshes,
with red-winged blackbirds, with his dog,
and with his stories untold.

Geese Over the Fall Canvas

Fall leaves gather in wispy piles
along the hiking trail
As cumulus clouds quilt patches over
the clear blue sky.
Breaks of sun brighten blazing golds,
and warm the morning breeze.
You stop to rest on the hillside,
reflecting on the beauty of solidarity
with changing season—
As the geese take flight
with stirring call over the fall canvas
and still lake water.

Fall Season in the Suburbs

Truth and beauty are harvested
in late October—
As you pause with crisp
and sullen morning air.
The squirrel gathers winter store
with seedlings and acorns scattered
by curbsides.
The trees are dappled with colour
And early mist burns off
with rising sun—
The call of wild geese distant
in crystal skies.

Fall Trail

The rustic tones of fall
stir reflection
As seeds spiral in the breeze
and scatter on path.
Fall is the best season for
long walks.
There is faith in hope
And faith in the beauty
of changing season.

Meadow Crow

The pine stands in morning mist
And damp poplar leaves bed
the back trail.
The air is cool and brisk.
Wild grasses wave to and fro
in morning breeze—
As thought is given to how
busy days pass with season—
The meadow crow caws
incessantly from the field.
Stirring auburn tones
of harmony.

Golden Leaves

The golden leaves dance in the light fall breeze
And lake waters are no longer hidden beyond bush
along the front road.
The wooden bridge to cemetery isle
is golden tresselled with sunbeam
breaking beyond cloud.
The distant lake water remains solemn slate
while diamonds surface on gentle crests of breaking waves
shoring bits of sun.
The wearied soul passing by on the lakefront road
takes a moment to rest under skies
and falling leaves.

Fair Trade Coffee Shop

I caught your knowing glance
As chatter rose over the poet's reading
The patrons coming and going with
the wafting aroma of roasted beans
and fair trade coffee.
The late morning was brisk with autumn
and leaves lightly whisked and tumbled
along the curbside of the artisan district.
It's no accident we met as banter perked
with the stimulant of caffeine.
The world is a less lonely place with
fair trade coffee.
And I am less lonely having met you—
another soul who loves coffee
and fall colours.

Reflection in the Window

Somewhere between the dark
and the light,
in the early hours before
the world gets busy,
when the stars are hidden
waiting for dawn
and the air is heavy with silence,
there is peace.
You gaze at your reflection
in the window with morning commute,
the city lights passing beyond
gathered thought—
All are toiling in the garden of life.
And times change as
the dark-eyed junco lodges
with morning chill and healthy feed
in the red berried
shrubbery.

The Winding Road

You rest by the stream
on the hillside as the sun sets
with fall colours.
And you're reminded how
beautiful life is on the
winding road—
Knowing the destination
is the beginning of
the journey.

Dormant Branches

The trees are barren
and dusty leaves cling
to dormant branches.
The speckled starlings
and royal grackles
mill about the yard.
Take flight blackbirds
with the chill
of changing season.
Take flight and revisit when
the spring song beckons.

Wintering Blue Jay

The wintering jay skirts in flight
And takes refuge in the scented boughs
of the tall pine.
White birches are bare, with chilled air
and sleet under desolate skies.
The sharp note of the jay
chastises hardened hearts—
from branches of spruce
with hoar frost and
ice palisades.

Weathered Crosses

Glistening woods border weathered crosses
with leanings cast from frozen ground.
The morning air, white and silent, clouds the steel sky.
The sun's etched disc melts ice around its pocket.
Beyond the woods, frosted glisten, a crunch of snow afoot
with pause by passer-by,
to breathe the moment and spy the raven atop the pine
with brazen breast barren to the northern wind.

A Solitary Note

On a frosted wooded break of day,
the white birches and grey poplars
stand barren against November greys;
the sprigs and twigs of branches
hedged with the evening's first snow
arch over the wooded heavens.
Along the pond's stilled edge, wedges of golden grass
crop through wintered drifts where
leaning aged posts run aside frozen fields,
the barbed fencing enclosing the broken sod.
All is still and bleak and chilled
when the tawned little sparrow, perched
on the lone branch of the barren birch,
rustles his soft brown down for warmth.
And heard is a melodious solitary note,
a lone little chirp, his hope
to meet his mate, after wintering the worst,
to scale with in harmony.

Wintered Countryside

The child clutches
the stuffed bear,
under a blanket
of stars
over the wintered
countryside.
The mother weeps.
Hope is veiled
with grief,
and harmony net
in prayer for peace.

Winter Walking Trail

The full moon suspends above the winter trail
from an open pocket of silver clouding.
The dog on evening walk gazes towards
the edge of the woods, and frosted hollow.
The trail ends by the quiet crescent
where fencing leans with fallen rails.
Spring greens of rock gardens are dormant
under crystal snow.
And windows flash with iridescent glow
With a dash of lights from season past.
The gardener yearns for spring
amidst the diamond frost—
And a distant bark is heard.
Then all is silent on the winter walk.

White Snow Geese

A moment with divinity
is when the white snow geese
pass overhead in flight
against the crystal azure
blue sky.

Black Capped Chickadee

The black capped
chickadees
string pure notes
of greeting
from the snow ladened
boughs of cedar.
I must get out
in crisp and cold air
to find joy in the day
As you, robust little
chickadee.

Season Snowfall

The evening is bright
with light snow falling at dusk—
blanketing our world with delight.
Shall we venture out together
into winter hinterland—
And enjoy a camper's mug
of hot chocolate?
Or just gaze out at the beauty of
the evening's snow
And snuggle under a cabin fleece throw
As we reflect on our plans
for the holidays.

SEASON OF OLD

The night is bright with stars above,
and the soft blanket of snow
reflects hope.
Goodwill is packaged fruit cake.
And handbells resonate
singular notes
of old faith.

Candles are cupped by carolers
with hope,
as flurries blanket frozen hills.
Children are bundled
with bright scarves.
Pulling sleds
and lacing skates.

The snow falls lightly
as the evening wears on.
And children's cheeks are rosy,
as they cozy under plaid throws
with mitts wrapped around
steaming mugs.

Children are tucked in for the night
with promise of reindeer
prancing on roofs.
And with cookies left out on plates.
The points of constellations
sparkle in the night sky
which is now clear.

Pause is given to the year past
with snow drifts on front steps.
Greeting cards refrain peace on earth
and goodwill.
Mitts with strings are hung to dry
like musical notes on lines
under the night sky.

The Donkey

The small donkey
that carried Mary
with child
into Bethlehem
knew the weight
of his burden.
You too, my child,
know the weight
of burden with
His plans for
you.
Be blessed.

Sprigs of Holly

Snow brings nostalgia
for season past—
With street lamps aglow
And snowflakes blanketing
the parkway path.
French pane windows
with decorative wreaths
Carollers with sheet notes
of goodwill and peace.
And baskets with sprigs
of holly.

The Red Mailbox

There is a
Christmas card
in the red mailbox
posted to you
Capped with an
angel's dusting
of snow
and holly.

Forecast of Snow

Snowflakes reflect in
pewter skies with dawn
As I let my dog out
to frolic in the yard.
And curl up with a book
to read.
The snow softly blankets
the quiet hours
And snow angels
imprint with forecast
of joy and magical
peace.

Snow Globe

Your calico cat
curls on the mat
in front of the warmth
of the fireplace
And dreams
of the magical world
of the snow globe
on the mantel.

Candlelight Service

The new year promises
precious moments
As I take your frail hand
And you worry about
plans for the season.
You wrap your scarf
over your top coat
The white pine branches
weighted with snow.
Handbells ring in crystal air
with starlit skies.
Homeward bound
Bearing candles into
the night.

OLD FATHER TIME

There is a lull in the season
before the new year
With a feeling of content
of time well spent with family
and friends—
You sit by the fireplace
and marvel
at old Father Time.
How yet another season passes
into a new calendar year—
And at how, as time passes,
blessings are the simpler
things in life.

Snow and Thistles

The silent snow blankets
the field of purple thistles
And reflects the light
of early hours.
The jay calls from the pine
in the morning frost
Before visiting the
winter feeder.

Quarter Note

The question of
empathy
and the well-being
of humanity
is hung from
a quarter note
suspended
in the slate steel
sky.

Joy

There is not much
gain in this world—
But of the intangible
shared in moments
of joy.

Sit for Tea

I want to sit with you over green,
mint or apple cinnamon tea,
and maybe a gingersnap or two.
And talk about the small stuff,
like how I spotted a wintering robin
on my walk with the dog today.
Let's rest.
And be grateful for the day.
As tomorrow's worries
will still be here
after tea.

A Poet and Picker and Friends

Let's drive to the snow-capped mountains,
in my Volkswagen van
which is decaled with stickers
of daisies and peace signs.
And, I will bring my picker friend.
He can pick tunes of Beatles and Dylan.
As the wood crackles, and the guitar glows.
And the campfire casts light
and shadows
under the stars.

Company in the Corner

The ghosts of great poets
sit on hardwood chairs
for the reading of my chapbook,
in the corner with arts and letters.
Poetry was read in smoky cafes
in their day.
There is a dignified air with
a shadow of a fedora—
And bemused curiosity.
Come out to Poet's Corner.
Come out and find me.
And I will find you.

Serenity

Awaken and be still.
Listen to the whisper of peace
on the breeze—
As you brood over intentions
unsettled—
Awaken and be still knowing
all is well.

Cherished Moments

The struggle of life is brief
and with the saddest moments
we are blessed.
The cherished moments are few—
too few shared but no
less precious.

Reclamation

Faith and
hope
with shafts
of light
renew with
your path.

Simply Love

I love mornings and songbirds,
park benches and crystal lakes,
mountains and mist,
dogs and long walks,
good neigbours, good friends,
a good book, a good song,
poetry and family.

Tribute

The gentleman wraps his coat
over his frame, and
the wind whistles as he sits
on the bench across from his home.

He ruminates that the ways
of the world do not appeal
to goodness and finer senses.

And in solitude, he searches,
as the sleet and rain
weight the bedding
for the frozen season.

The pair of crows caw before
shadow of flight.

His echoing resonance
in lyric and song
is prophetic brokenness
of times.

And carried in the wind
is the hallowed refrain.
Hallelujah.

Praise Thy Seasons

At the end of the road taken,
if the day's troubles
bring dark fringes to my spirit,
by praising the Lord for all of His goodness,
my heart will abound in joy
and my spirit in gladness.
Praise for the beauty found in each day.

And at the end of the road travelled,
praise for each path sought and not taken,
for it is better if not of my own accord
as I may then be led with guidance.

And on my travels may I take time to pause—
to smell the crisp stilled air on a September morn
when the green grass is settled with morning dew,
and the birds are singing of the end of the season
with the breaking of a new dawn.

And may I pause in the stillness of a winter night,
when the silver moon suspends high over the crispness,
and the frost glistens on the white birch horizons.

And may I pause in the stillness of the dew on an early spring morn,
when the wild flower by the mossy stone yawns and stretches
its lavender petals under the warm caress of the morning sun.

And may I pause under the stillness of a hot summer day,
when my bare feet are cooled by the grainy beach sands
and washed in the cool waters of the ebb and flow.
And in stillness, may I pause to reflect on the beauty
that I passed in hurried moments,
as I may know Him through praising the beauty
found in each day of each season.
And I may see Him in this beauty.

Praise for the beauty found in each day.
And if burdened in moments of silence,
I may know that I am not alone on the road—
And through all trials and tribulations,
I may know of His gentleness, may know of His wisdom,
and may have His forgiveness.
Praise for the beauty found in each day.

Greet the Day

Goodbyes are not simple.
Greet the new day with
the winter songbird as you
count your blessings.
And stay well until
we meet again.

Index of Opening Phrases

A moment with divinity [57]
A note is tucked under the amethyst [35]
Almost every wound heals as time passes [18]
At the end of the road taken [81]
Awaken and be still [75]
Dark clouds hide away the stars [38]
Early each dawn before the bustling city day [19]
Faith and hope with shafts of light renew [77]
Fall leaves gather in wispy piles along the hiking trail [43]
Friendships are made as we sit in the shade [32]
Glistening woods border weathered crosses [53]
Goodbyes are not simple [83]
He returned to the park, the evening chilled [42]
Hey Dylan, drop over, so we can discuss current events [20]
I am told the rare sighting of the blue heron is a blessing [13]
I bravely stepped up to the prairie town church [33]
I caught your knowing glance [48]
I hear the rain patter outside of my window [9]
I harvest cloves of harmony in my soul [40]
I love mornings and songbirds [78]
I miss you over morning coffee [22]
I thought of you today with broken longing [12]
I want to sit with you over green, mint or apple cinnamon tea [72]

In front of my childhood home [41]
Just as the crow awakens the songbird [16]
Last summer we sat in the shade of the birch tree [21]
Let's drive to the snow-capped mountains [73]
On a frosted wooded break of day [54]
On the rocks. As golden as the sunset [34]
Petals of he loves me, loves me not, line diverging pathways [15]
Small birds shelter with no song [2]
Snow brings nostalgia for season past [63]
Snowflakes reflect in pewter skies with dawn [65]
Someone is knocking at the door in the early morning hours [4]
Somewhere between the dark and the light [49]
Strolling along coastal shores, sandpipers dash on the beach [10]
The black capped chickadees string pure notes of greeting [58]
The child clutches the stuffed bear, under a blanket of stars [55]
The day awakens from slumber [7]
The dove descended in haze of a morning dream [1]
The evening is bright with light snow falling at dusk [59]
The full moon suspends above the winter trail [56]
The gentleman wraps his coat over his frame [79]
The ghosts of great poets sit on hardwood chairs [74]
The golden leaves dance in the light fall breeze [47]
The logger planned to paddle cross the lake to fly-fish [25]
The mist rises over the hazed mountain [26]
The new year promises precious moments [67]
The night is bright with stars above [60]
The offshore landing is framed with weathered logs [27]
The pine stands in morning mist [46]
The planet groans as if in labour pain [28]
The question of empathy [70]
The robin sits under the sun on the manicured lawn [23]
The rustic tones of fall stir reflection [45]
The scent of white clover lends sweetness to the breeze [5]
The silent snow blankets the field of purple thistles [69]

The small donkey that carried Mary with child [62]
The snow falls lightly with the month of April [8]
The soul deepens with sorrow like water in the still pool on the bend of the river [24]
The steel sky darkens the forest floor [39]
The struggle of life is brief [76]
The trees are barren and dusty leaves cling to dormant branches [51]
The white caps splash over the rocky crag [11]
The white-throated sparrow nests in the light spring rain [6]
The wintering jay skirts in flight [52]
There is a Christmas card in the red mailbox [64]
There is a lull in the season before the new year [68]
There is not much to gain in this world [71]
Travel with the good with the beginning of a new journey [37]
Trust the ebb and flow of life [3]
Truth and beauty are harvested in late October [44]
We look out at our world with a jade tint to our lens [31]
Weep, weep, for our brothers and sisters [17]
What took you so long? [36]
With early dawn I stood by the bay [14]
With fame and fortune we shall fly to Paris [30]
You rest by the stream on the hillside [50]
Your calico cat curls on the mat [66]

About the Author

Terry-Lynn Johnson is a poet, essayist, lyricist and educator. She is published with The Victorian Web and The Thomas Hardy Society. Her favourite authors are Leonard Cohen, Ernest Hemingway and Maya Angelou with an interest in romantic, Victorian and modernist poetry.

Her first collection of poetry *Sprigs and Twigs: A Solitary Note & Selected Poems (Collector's Edition)* was published with FriesenPress (October 2021).

She was born in Nipigon, Ontario.

She attained an Honours Bachelor of Arts in Social Sciences and Humanities at Lakehead University. She also attained a Bachelor of Education and Master of Education at Lakehead University.

She has a son and daughter with two grandchildren. Her husband is a professional musician and together they perform acoustic music and poetry at a variety of venues. Their home is in northwestern Ontario on the shores of Lake Superior.

www.ingramcontent.com/pod-product-compliance
Lightning Source LLC
LaVergne TN
LVHW020936090426
835512LV00020B/3389